Contents

Galileo

Brandon Robshaw and Rochelle Scholar

Published in association with The Basic Skills Agency

Hodder & Stoughton

A MEMBER OF THE HODDER HEADLINE GROUP

Acknowledgements

Cover: Darren Lock/The Organisation.

Illustrations: Mike Bell.

Painting on p. 26 of Galileo by Justus Sustermans, from the Galleria degli Uffizi, Florence (Photo: AKG).

Orders: please contact Bookpoint Ltd, 39 Milton Park, Abingdon, Oxon OX14 4TD. Telephone: (44) 01235 400414, Fax: (44) 01235 400454. Lines are open from 9.00–6.00, Monday to Saturday, with a 24 hour message answering service. Email address: orders@bookpoint.co.uk

British Library Cataloguing in Publication Data
A catalogue record for this title is available from The British Library

ISBN 0 340 74269 0

First published 1999
Impression number   10 9 8 7 6 5 4 3 2 1
Year   2004 2003 2002 2001 2000 1999

Copyright © 1999 Brandon Robshaw and Rochelle Scholar

Typeset by Fakenham Photosetting Ltd, Fakenham, Norfolk.
Printed in Great Britain for Hodder & Stoughton Educational, a division of Hodder Headline Plc, 338 Euston Road, London NW1 3BH by Redwood Books, Trowbridge, Wiltshire.

1 The Letter

Galileo was worried.
Very worried.

You didn't mess
with the Inquisition.
People who messed
with the Inquisition
ended up dead.

The Inquisition made sure
that people believed the right things.
You had to believe
what the Church believed.
If you didn't,
you were punished.
And the punishment
was death by burning.

They didn't burn you to death
straight away.
They tortured you first.
They crushed your thumbs
in the thumb-screw.
They burnt your flesh
with red hot irons.
They stretched your body
on the rack.
Finally, they burnt you alive.

Galileo looked at the letter in his hand.
It was from the Inquisition.
They wanted him to go to Rome.
They had some questions to ask him.

Galileo was worried.
Very worried.

2 Galileo's Book

Galileo lived in Florence,
nearly 200 miles from Rome.
This was a long journey
in the days before cars or trains.
Galileo was an old man.
He was not well.

He tried writing to the Inquisition.
He said he was too ill
to make the journey.
But you couldn't say no
to the Inquisition.
They told him
he had to come to Rome – or else.

In 1633,
Galileo made the journey to Rome.
When he arrived,
he expected to be put in prison.
But Galileo was a famous scientist.
They gave him special treatment.
They let him stay in a pleasant house
with a garden.
The house was watched
to stop him escaping.

The first day of Galileo's trial began.
He stood before the Inquisition –
stern-faced men in black robes.
The Chief Inquisitor
fixed him with cold eyes.

'Do you know why you are here?'
he asked.

'Yes,' said Galileo quietly.

'Why?'

'Because of my book –
Dialogue on the Great World Systems.'

'That's right.
And what about your book?'

'It says the Earth
moves round the Sun.'

'Yes. But that's not what it says
in the Bible, is it?'

'No.'

'In the Bible, it says
the Earth stands still, doesn't it?'

'Yes.'

'So to say different
is a crime, isn't it?'

Galileo's lips were dry.
'Yes,' he said.

'But perhaps you made a mistake?'
said the Chief Inquisitor.
'Perhaps your book was wrong.'

Galileo saw what was happening.
They were giving him a chance
to save his life.
If he said his book was all a mistake,
he would be safe.
But the book was his life's work.
It was a terrible choice.
Deny his life's work –
or be burnt to death.

3 Early Life

Galileo was born 70 years earlier,
in Pisa in 1564.
His father was a musician.
The family moved to Florence
when Galileo was ten.

Galileo was taught by the monks
in a nearby monastery.
He was a bright child
and learned very quickly.

At the age of 17
he went to the University of Pisa
to study medicine.
He wanted to become a doctor.
But while he was there
he changed his mind.
He became interested in nature and science.

Galileo was interested
in the world around him
and the way it worked.
He noticed everything.

One day, he noticed a lamp swinging
in Pisa cathedral.
He noticed that
as the swing got shorter,
it got slower.
Whether the swing was long or short,
it took the same time.
Many years later,
Galileo remembered this.
It gave him the idea for a pendulum
that would help clocks keep better time.

He began to study mathematics.
He showed such talent
that he became
Lecturer in Mathematics at Pisa.
He was still only 25.

4 Looking and Seeing

Galileo believed
that to make discoveries in science,
you had to use your eyes.
It wasn't enough to have a theory.
You had to look and see what happened.

Galileo discovered
a new law about how things fall.
People used to think
that heavy objects fell faster than light ones.
Galileo showed that they fall at the same speed.
The story goes that he went to the top
of the Tower of Pisa
and dropped different weights off.
They all hit the ground at the same time.

Galileo became quite famous.
But his job at Pisa
was not well paid.
In 1592, he applied for a job
as Professor of Mathematics
at the University of Padua.
He got the job.
It was much better paid.

Galileo spent the next 18 years at Padua.
He did most of his best work there.

In 1604, he proved
that falling objects always speed up
at the same rate.
He also proved that a ball
thrown into the air
falls in a curve.

These discoveries came
from Galileo's method of science –
carry out tests and check the results.

A new tool had just been invented
to help scientists with their work.
It was the telescope.

5 The Telescope

The first telescopes
were not very powerful.
They were little more than toys.

Galileo built a new, improved telescope.
It made things look 32 times larger.
It was the first telescope
powerful enough to study the stars.

With his new telescope,
Galileo began to study the night sky.
He made many new discoveries.

He was the first person to discover
that the Moon was full of craters
and mountains.
People used to think that the Moon was smooth.

He discovered the moons of Jupiter.
He discovered that the Milky Way
was a collection of stars.

Galileo made many great discoveries.
But he also claimed credit for discoveries
that were not his own.
He claimed that he was the first person
to discover spots on the surface of the Sun.
In fact, others had already noticed them
and published their findings.

Another scientist, Kepler, made a discovery
about the movement of the planets.
Everyone thought they moved in circles.
Kepler said they moved in ovals.
He was right.
Galileo ignored this completely.
Perhaps it was because
he had not discovered it himself.

Galileo wanted the credit for everything.
He once wrote:
'It was granted to me alone
to discover all the new wonders in the sky
and nothing to anybody else.'

He was a brilliant man,
but also a very vain one.

6 A Warning

Galileo was not the first person to say
that the Earth goes round the Sun.
A scientist called Copernicus
had said it nearly 100 years earlier.

But it was still dangerous to say so.
It went against the Bible.
The Inquisition did not approve.

You were allowed to say it as a theory.
You could say,
'*What if* the Earth went round the Sun?'
You could not argue
that it was definitely true.

In 1613, Galileo published three letters
on his discoveries.
In them, he said that Copernicus was right.
The Earth went round the Sun.

At once, the Inquisition
were on the case.
They warned Galileo to stop.
They said he could discuss
Copernicus's theory.
But he must not teach
that it was true.

Galileo was scared.
He knew what the Inquisition could do.
He decided to keep quiet.

He moved to Florence.
He lived quietly there.
He stopped publishing his ideas.

But Galileo knew he was right.
He wanted the whole world
to know he was right.
He could not keep quiet forever.

In 1624, a new Pope was elected.
Galileo went to see him in Rome.
The new Pope seemed friendly to Galileo.
Galileo thought it would at last be safe
to publish his ideas.

He set to work on his great book.
It was called
Dialogue on the Great World Systems.
In it, he said that all the planets
– including the Earth –
went round the Sun.

The book came out in 1630.
At once, Galileo was in trouble.
The Inquisition ordered him to Rome.
They said they had
some questions to ask him.

7 'But It Does Move'

'Perhaps your book was wrong,'
said the Chief Inquisitor.
'Or perhaps you didn't really mean it.'

Galileo was silent.
The Inquisitors in their black robes
stared at him.

Galileo knew he was right.
He also knew he didn't want
to be tortured and burned to death.

'You're right – I didn't really mean it,'
he said at last.
'I wrote that book to show
that Copernicus was wrong.
It was all a misunderstanding.'

'So the Earth doesn't move?'
said the Chief Inquisitor.

'That's right,' said Galileo.
'It doesn't move.'

As Galileo was led from the room,
he said under his breath:
'But it does move.'
Luckily for him,
the Inquisitors did not hear.

8 The Last Years

Galileo had saved his life.
There would be no torture,
no burning at the stake for him.

Today, everyone knows
that Galileo was right.
The Earth does go round the Sun.
Galileo knew he was right.
But he didn't have much choice.
He had to deny it to save his life.

He was still punished, though.
The Inquisition sentenced him
to prison.
The Pope, however, changed the sentence
to house arrest.
Galileo went back to his house in Florence.
He was allowed to live there in peace.
But he was not allowed to travel.

Galileo lived another eight years.
He still did scientific work.
He wrote a book on mechanics,
The Two New Sciences.
For a while, he carried on
studying the skies.
Sadly, in 1637 he went blind.
He would make no more discoveries
with his telescope.

In his last years,
he remembered the swinging lamp
he had seen as a student.
He had the idea for a pendulum
that would help clocks keep better time.
He wrote notes for this idea.

Galileo died of a fever in 1642.

The pendulum clock was built
a few years after Galileo's death
by a Dutch scientist.
It worked perfectly.

Galileo, painted in 1636.

Galileo's Life

15 February 1564   Galileo Galilei born in Pisa

1581   Enters University of Pisa

1592   Becomes Professor of Mathematics
at Padua

1604   Does work on speed of falling objects

1610   Makes series of discoveries
about the stars and planets

1613   First states his belief
that the Earth goes round the Sun.
He is warned by the Church
not to teach this theory as true.

1630   Publishes *Dialogue on the Great World Systems*

1633   Called to Rome by the Inquisition.
He is forced to deny his theory that
the Earth goes round the Sun.
He is put under house arrest.

1634   Publishes *Two New Sciences*

1637   Goes blind

8 January 1642   Galileo dies